BABY LEARNING THROUGH BABY PLAY

A Parent's Guide for the First Two Years

BABY LEARNING THROUGH BABY PLAY

A Parent's Guide for the First Two Years

Ira J. Gordon

Institute for Development of Human Resources
University of Florida
Gainesville, Florida

Illustrations and Design by
David Smiton and Norman Kramer

ST. MARTIN'S PRESS
New York

To my wife Esther and our children Gary and Bonnie

The materials in this book reflect the author's research which has been supported in part by the Fund for the Advancement of Education, the Children's Bureau, and the National Institute of Mental Health. Special thanks are due to the author's graduate students, especially J. Ronald Lally.

For information, write:

St. Martin's Press, Inc.,

175 Fifth Ave., New York, N.Y. 10010

Manufactured in the United States of America

Library of Congress Catalog Card Number: 73-125310

AFFILIATED PUBLISHERS:

Macmillan & Company, Limited, London—

also at Bombay, Calcutta, Madras and Melbourne—

The Macmillan Company of Canada, Limited, Toronto

Contents

CONCLUSION

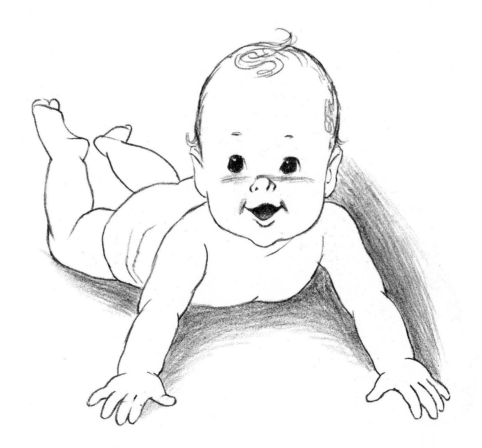

2

To the Parents

Most parents dream great dreams for their children. They want them to be happy and successful in their work and their home lives, but they know that, in spite of the song, wishing will not make it so. The question they ask is, "What *will* make it so?" or, more answerably, "What will *help* make it so?"

This book tries to give you some things that are likely to help. There is no guarantee, but the latest research in child development strongly suggests that there are experiences you can provide your baby—experiences in the form of games and play—that will greatly influence his intellectual ability later on. Expressing it the other way around, we can now say that if certain kinds of experiences are *not* provided for a baby during the first two years of his life, the chances of his reaching the intellectual potential he was born with are probably reduced.

This means that if you take two babies born with equal natural gifts and leave one to lie in his crib for hundreds of hours staring at a blank ceiling while the other is engaged in all sorts of interesting, enjoyable and intellectually stimulating play, the second baby will build an advantage that will pay off in school and throughout his life.

The bright side of what research has to tell us is this: The most helpful sorts of experiences for your baby are not only easy for you to supply, but are great fun for both you and him, and they have all sorts of added benefits as side-effects.

The games described in this book are designed to do several things. *First*, they will help the baby develop basic skills such as focusing the eyes, coordinating the eye and hand, distinguishing differences among almost identical objects—skills that will have an immediate pay-off in fun, and a later pay-off in the ability to perform more complicated jobs such as reading and thinking.

Second, and perhaps even more vital, once he has these basic skills, he needs to become aware of how the skills can be useful in exploring the world around him. That is, he needs *to learn to learn*—and the games are devised to help him do this. This is something beyond the mere acquisition of facts. It's an attitude about new situations and an approach to dealing with them.

Third, your baby will learn that learning is enjoyable. He will have fun learning. He will get satisfaction not only from the activity itself, but also from the results—his increase in ability to handle his world. This leads to the *fourth* outcome.

The games will also impart to the baby some basic facts about himself and the world around him. The sooner he has the impression the world is an orderly, consistent, interesting and (to a certain extent) controllable place, the sooner will he have a confidence that is essential to many aspects of life, but in particular to the inclination to explore—that is, to learn.

Fourth, this confidence about what he is and what he can do will be enhanced mightily by his growing trust in you. The great majority of the play in this book calls for an interaction between him and you, and this interaction—which is conveying to him your dependability and good will—is fully as important as the game itself. This is the foundation of a loving relationship that can last all your lives together, and, in fact, that can affect his relationships with all the people he'll ever meet.

Another great benefit of the play can be the way it builds in you a sense of joy, love and accomplishment with your child.

You'll have a feeling of participating so much more in his growth, rather than just observing. But even your observing will improve, bringing with it immediate excitement, and in the long run a much richer store of memories.

The games are arranged in very rough order of difficulty, and in an order of decreasing control of the play by you and increasing control by your child. The order has to be rough because if there's anything we know about children it's that no two are exactly alike. They show a delightful disparity, and this means there is no need to try—indeed, there's a need *not* to try—to make your baby fit any rigid schedules or sequences or performance levels. Take your cues from the baby himself, and remember always the key word is *play*. He'll enjoy lots of these games, but probably not all of them, and there's no necessity for him to play at any unless he finds it fun.

An important part of the aim here is to foster a happy attitude toward exploratory activity, and the general rule to follow as you go through the book is: Encourage him to do everything, but force him to do nothing.

It takes experience, in tandem with maturation, for readiness for learning to develop. Experience creates readiness, it just does not come about. Based upon both his growth and his background of experience, your baby will show you, by his actions, that he is ready for new games. It is important that you do not pressure him for performance before he is ready.

One safeguard against such pressure is to be sure that you have fun with the play, too. If you attack it with a grim, joyless determination to see the baby "succeed", the mood will be conveyed to him and a good deal will be lost. The games aren't tests, and the baby mustn't be called on to "pass" any of them.

These games are *not* a curriculum. This is not a set of lesson plans, but suggestions and ideas for enhancing development. There are many ways to provide experience, there are no fixed "tasks," and no notion that, if your child does not progress smoothly, page by page, he will be doomed. The basic principle is that you should provide him with many interesting opportunities to learn, to explore, to interact with you.

The suggestions in this book are the result of a long and intensive search for those activities that will bring the most to your baby—in fun, instruction, interest, and confidence in himself and you. Despite the systematic study that has gone into it, you'll find that much of it is already familiar to you. Your own mother, without any help from a child psychologist, probably played many of these same games with you. And you probably would have hit on much of the rest of the book on your own. But to me it is encouraging rather than deflating to discover, after long labor, that pat-a-cake is a good game to play with your child. I hope it encourages you too, because I want you to feel free to invent and improvise, think up your own variations and altogether new things to do.

The book may have some things in it that you would not have hit on—at least, not at the age levels recommended here—but nevertheless I think of it only as a beginning, a starting point for you and your baby, something that will enable you to give him an early, deserved helping-hand in fulfilling the promise he was born with. Everything after, a lifetime of creative playing and living together, will come not from any book but from you and from your child.

GAMES FOR THE EARLY MONTHS

These first games can be started when your baby is about three months old and his usual position is flat on his back or his stomach. They're designed to help him use his new-found ability to make sounds and move his head and hands at will.

These early sounds are the first step toward language. He's using them to express happy feelings of pleasure, eagerness, and satisfaction, and also to show his discomfort. By four months or so he responds to his mother's voice, and by six months he imitates other people's sounds and babble.

The key thing at this stage is to let him know that his efforts are having an effect: When he makes a sound, he gets a pleasant response; when he turns his head toward the noise of the rattle he *sees* it, and when he reaches for it he can touch it, and even hold it. It's important that these early reachings out—with his voice and his eyes and his hands—bring him a payoff. It's important, first, because he enjoys it, and second, because he needs this encouragement, this feeling that the world *is* explorable, this assurance that he can make things happen. Imagine the effect on an infant's confidence and willingness to continue to reach out to the world if these early efforts never bring a response—if, in other words, he comes to feel that nothing he does makes any difference.

Read through the whole section first; see where you want to start. Although the "conversation" activity is placed first, most children respond to the other activities before they do much with this one. Remember, no two babies are quite the same. Each baby's pace and taste is his own alone.

Dialogue — 1

"Dialogue" is designed to promote his speech soundmaking. This wins him new attention and interest, brings you and him closer together, and begins language development.

When you're diapering, bathing, or holding the baby, or just watching him lie in his crib looking around, if he makes a sound like a coo or a gurgle, respond to him by a combination of stroking his stomach, moving your head close enough and smiling so you're sure he sees you, and repeating the sound he makes. He may then coo some more and you have a "conversation" going. This may be a very brief encounter that either you or he can break off. It's easy to repeat and can be done at odd moments any time.

9

On the Track of the Rattle

These rattle games are in a sequence and are designed to foster the coordination of the baby's senses (eyes and ears) with his ability to move. The baby's control over his own body develops from the head down. He has control over his head before he can use his arms and much before he can use his legs. He is able to focus his eyes and can detect a wide variety of sounds. With the rattle games, we can tie sight, sound and movement together. Early success at these coordinated efforts increases his ability to manage more complex efforts later on. In particular, it seems to have an effect on eventual reading ability.

All of the rattle games can be played by any adult, or an older brother or sister, and they can be tried any time the baby feels playful and as often as it amuses him. Even if he can do the harder ones, it's fun and worthwhile to go back and let him practice the easier ones. When he does succeed at one of the games, don't think of it as his having "passed that test" and now it's time to go on to the next one. Children enjoy repetition, and they get something out of it each time because coordination is a skill that improves with practice.

MOBILES are very useful "extra added attractions" while your baby is in the crib. He can practice using his eyes to follow the bright, moving objects as they swing and turn. Babies will spend more time looking at something which is involved (has lots of light and dark and movement in it) than a very simple object.

You may want to hang bright, bold, colorful pictures where the baby can see them.

When the baby is lying in his crib, or on a rug on the floor, or on any flat, safe place, stand behind him so that you are out of his line of sight and hold a rattle about a foot above his face. Shake it gently until he looks at it.

When you're sure he sees it, move the rattle in a slow circle around the baby's head so that he can keep it in sight by just moving his eyes without moving his head. For convenience, you may want to gently hold the baby by placing your hand on his stomach.

After he follows it for awhile, try reversing directions, going the other way around the circle—always smoothly and slowly. Boys seem to "follow" sooner than girls.

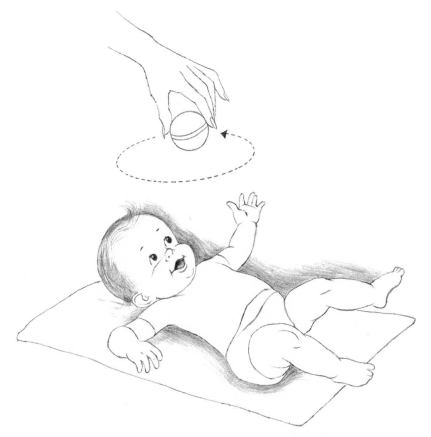

After the baby has had practice and enjoyment in following only with his eyes, hold the rattle above his head about 12 inches from his eyes and move it in a curved line all the way down to the side so that he has to turn his head to follow the sound. Now he has to put his eyes and his head to work. Then go in the other direction so that he gets practice in moving his head both ways.

If he reaches for the rattle or accidentally grabs it with his hand, let him have it, even if he puts it in his mouth.

While you're doing this you should begin to surround him with what I call a "language envelope"—that is, talk gently to him and describe what you're doing, even though he obviously doesn't understand the words. The sound of your voice, its rhythm and pattern, will in the long run contribute to language learning.

After the baby can "use his head," make him work harder to see the rattle. Continue to keep your body mostly out of his sight so that he has to attend to the sound rather than you. Shake the rattle a little behind his head.

If his eyes look up, but he can't see it, bring it over his head into view and then move it back out of sight until he tries to move his head so he can see it. He has to push his head back to see, and when he does, you can say cheerfully "*now* you see it."

Try this on both the right and left sides of his head. If he reaches for the rattle let him grab it and play with it, then gently repeat the game.

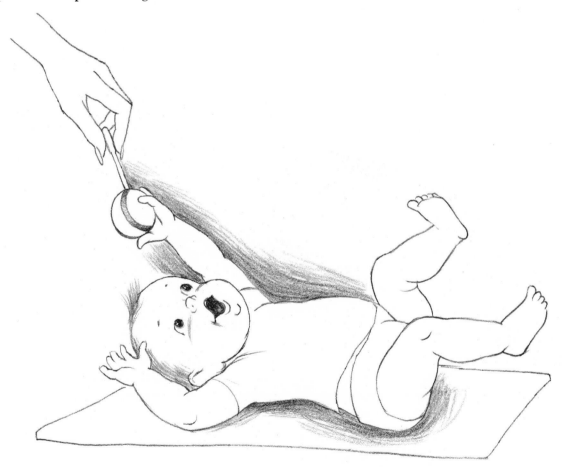

Another rattle game can be played when your baby is lying on his stomach. Face him and dangle the rattle directly in front of his face. Slowly lift the object so that he has to raise his head to follow it. Encourage him, by helping or showing, to push up on his arms to keep the object in view. When he does, smile and then lower the rattle and repeat.

In this game he has to push his head up in a different direction from the previous one. He'll probably be a little older than when you played the first rattle game because he has to be able to support himself on his arms.

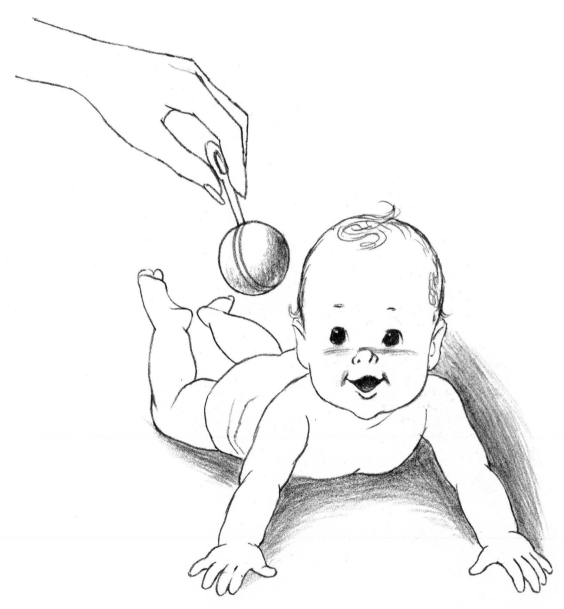

Boy Meets Toe

From about three months to about six or seven months your baby is beginning to sort out the world in simple ways. He is beginning to develop his sense of self, or self esteem, or identity. This is a fundamental part of all of us, and affects how we think and behave throughout our lives. At this stage, besides feeling comfortable because of the care and love he is receiving, the baby is starting to learn what is a part of him and what is not. This may seem like knowledge you're born with, but it's not; it's something you learn. Your baby will love to explore. When he examines an object by tasting or chewing it, he feels something in his mouth. When he sticks his big toe or thumb in his mouth and chews it, he feels something in two places. This is how he begins to discover his body. You help by giving lots of opportunities to explore many things so he can learn what's him and what's not.

Testing, Testing . . .

At this age the mouth is the best part of the body for testing because it's the most sensitive. Be sure the objects are safe for the mouth so that you don't encourage the child to explore on the one hand, and take things away from him and deny him on the other. He'll use his mouth to find out that things feel and taste differently.

Use common objects from around the house and leave a few of them with him at a time.

Talk to him about the objects; say their names and how they feel or taste. Remember the language envelope!

If he's in a safe place with safe objects you may leave them with him. Be sure they're too big for him to swallow.

Replace them with others so that he has something familiar and something new. He'll always be interested in new objects, and soon he'll be finding them on his own. Until he does, make sure you supply him with a changing inventory to play with.

Look Ma, No Hands!

Baby will be delighted to learn he can make some things happen, even when he can't touch them.

You can use either the cradle gym, or you can fasten a mobile to the crib, or you can tie some colorful pieces of cording or other fabrics to the top bar of the crib over the baby's feet, where he can see them.

Bounce the crib mattress with your hand near his feet to make the objects move.

Take one of his feet, and gently tap it on the mattress to set the objects in motion. He'll see that movements on the mattress cause an interesting action, and he can do it on his own, when he wants to.

Mount a CRADLE GYM on his crib. This will allow him to practice on his own any time he chooses. When you play the rattle game with him, he gets the combination of grasping an interesting object and interacting with a family member. The cradle gym gives him opportunity to practice his skill in getting hold of what he wants and making it move the way he wants. The mixture of your play with him and his play with the cradle gym gives him two kinds of learning experience.

Gotcha!

Now that your baby has learned to follow the rattle with his eyes and head, we can take the next step and use it as a toy he can grab. This coordination of eye and hand is an important step forward, and he will have fun taking it.

Hold the rattle about a foot over the baby's stomach and shake it until he notices it. Then, move it slowly down so it becomes possible for him to grab it as his arms reach up. Smile and say, "Get the rattle, grab it." When he does, say in an excited and happy tone, "You got it" or "Johnny got it." Let him pull it down toward him. Then gently move it up until he releases it and continue this back and forth between you and him, until he indicates he's had enough.

GAMES FOR THE SITTING AND "LAP" BABY

These games are for a baby of five or six months of age up to about nine months, when he is no longer confined to his back or stomach. They take advantage of the baby's increased ability to spot and reach objects in space, and they show him that when he does reach them he can make things happen to them—that is, when he acts on an object, it produces results. During these months he's improving his physical coordination and also his own sense of self. He now recognizes his mother as separate from him, and he's busy building trust in his parents and others around him.

He's also acquiring the new and important notion of dependability — that is, consistency of response from the people and the objective world around him. Babies live in the present, from moment to moment. They have little past, and they don't know there is a future. We adults owe some of our security to being able to predict things, and to our belief that certain things will be regular and orderly. The earlier the child acquires this same security the better off he is. The sooner he senses he is surrounded by an orderly, consistent and predictable world, the sooner he'll be comfortable in it, and the more willing and confident he'll be about exploring new things. We don't all arrive at adulthood with an equal, maximum amount of this willingness and confidence. If we believe that many attitudes — like aptitudes — are developed by a child in his earliest years (and never quite reach their full potential later if they're not developed then) then we want to see that our babies get off to a good start.

Language grows during this time from six months on. The baby produces speech sounds, enjoys imitating some adult sounds and begins to be able to follow simple directions. Although he usually doesn't use words himself, his behavior begins to show that he understands some of them. Remember, he'll learn language only if you use a good deal of it around him. Whenever you're with him, be sure to speak in sentences, make your voice rise and fall, get loud and soft, fast and slow. Surround the child at appropriate times with words. There are some suggestions at the end of this section for rhythm games and rhymes that are both fun and teach.

Two-way Stretch

The game's aim is to give your baby practice in controlling things around him by using his body. It follows "Grab the Rattle" and goes along with use of the cradle gym. By this time he can support himself in a sitting position and this extends his reach.

Take any kind of object that has some stretch and pull to it, or make a simple toy from a spool and a piece of elastic.

Dangle it near the baby and encourage him to reach and grab for it. Use such words as "get," "grab" and "catch" while you're playing together: "Grab the spool, Danny! Try to grab it! Grab it, Dan!"

When he does grasp it, pull gently away so there's some stretch between you and him. Get into a push-pull game with him. "Pull, Dan. You pull and I'll pull." Then, gently release it and repeat. Try it so that he uses both hands.

Be sure it's fun and *not* teasing. Keep the toy so that he can get it when he makes an effort. Remember that the underlying principle you want to convey to your baby is that it's worthwhile trying to do things, that an effort on his part can have gratifying results.

When he makes sounds of pleasure because he has grabbed it, respond to these sounds as you did at the very beginning—that is, make them back. Enjoy his enjoyment. When you do, you not only increase his desire to practice (and thus improve his skill), you also increase his sense of well-being through persuading him of your sympathy and good-will.

Scouting the Territory

Your baby now is able to explore many things with his eyes and hands as well as with his mouth. When you're outside together, let him reach and handle natural objects, such as rocks, leaves, sand, sticks, snow, pine cones. As he does so, describe what he's doing and the way things feel, as well as giving the things' names.

If he can get around under his own power, let him wander and explore — under your watchful eye.

Since he still may be using his mouth as a testing ground, be careful of what objects are around. Many babies like to pick up anything that's around, including used cigarette butts, tin cans, worms and the other things that find their way to or live on the ground. You might want to "police the area" first to be sure of what's there.

"Scouting" uses the child's natural curiosity, exposes him to a variety of materials so that later on it will be easier for him to sort materials into groups, a skill of great importance in math and science. It also aids his power of observing likes and differences which pays off in reading where he must be able to notice the difference between, say an "e" and a "c". Although he can't tell likes and differences yet, the more experience he has exploring, the easier that will come.

A follow-up set of activities to the natural exploration is to select some objects that share some characteristic — that is, get four or five hard things, four or five soft, four or five fuzzy.

Give the baby the various hard things and while he is handling them, talk about their hardness.

Do not deal with anything else. Stay with one fact.

Shift to another set of objects, such as soft, and stay with these for awhile. Nobody learns from one example. Certainly not the young child.

Present him with many things and don't be afraid of repetition. Let him play with the objects, any way he likes. At this stage you simply want to increase his range of experience. Your baby will learn many things, pick up many ideas, from sheer exposure. He doesn't always have to do something specific, and you don't always have to be a directive teacher, giving him lots of chances to handle new things is also teaching.

Think of other natural experiences that all of us share in which we learn to group things as alike because they have something in common. You can emphasize hot foods and cold foods, sweet foods and salty foods. The child will make connections between words and objects when he has a lot of experience with them and when some action is connected to them. As he eats something hot, talk about hot things. Call the water hot when it is so; and the radiator. As he handles things that are fuzzy, talk about fuzziness.

Don't drill on these words or expect him to say them. You're not trying to teach him the particular words but rather the general fact that words are used to describe and name things.

"Mirror, Mirror on the Wall . . ."

Earlier the child began to get a notion of himself from handling objects and parts of his body. Now he can enjoy another way; he can see himself. Place him comfortably on your lap and have him look in a hand mirror so that he can see himself. Say, "Look, there's Billy." "I see Billy here and I see Billy there." "Where's Billy?" Have him point to his own image in the mirror. Do this at various times, and you will notice he will begin to recognize himself. About a year from now he will play act in front of a mirror, striking poses, making faces.

You may even add on to this in time by pointing to parts of the body and naming them after you're sure that he recognizes the total as him.

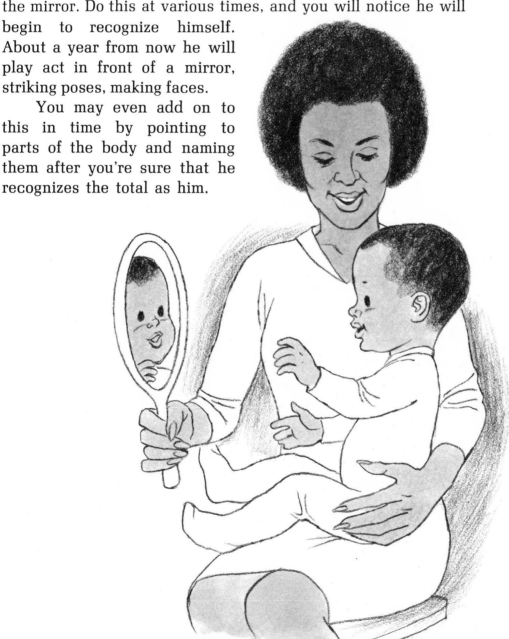

The mirror has other uses in addition to recognizing one's self. It can also be used to acquaint the baby with some fundamental facts about the three-dimensional world he lives in. One of them is the idea that objects have a location in space, and so does *he,* so that an object can be behind him.

Take a toy with which the baby is familiar and, while holding the baby on your lap, show him the reflection of the toy in the mirror.

Have him try to get the toy and see if he reaches toward the mirror or toward the real object. Remember, make a game of it. If he turns around, give him the toy.

Try this with several objects until the game becomes old and baby no longer enjoys it.

Caution: This is one game that it takes *two* to play. If it's a breakable glass mirror, do *not* leave it handy when you're not around.

The Rattle Rides Again

Earlier we used a rattle to get the baby to turn or lift his head in search of the source of sound. Now that he is able to sit up, and can handle himself better, he's ready to use not just his head but his whole trunk to track down his pesky friend.

Hold a rattle off to one side so that he can hear it but has to turn his whole body now from his sitting position to find it. After he's found where the sound is coming from, he will probably reach for the object. Give it to him and let him play with it.

Try this again at another time from the other direction. If you used the right side, now use the left. Girls seem to catch on to this game sooner than boys. Your daughter may enjoy trying this before any other experience in this series. However, each child has her own pattern!

Baby Power!

Now that the baby has absorbed the idea of using his own body to get what he wants, he's ready for games that call for using *other things* to get what he wants. These games increase his understanding of how the world works, help him to learn to do for himself, and add to his sense of pride. Your show of approval at his new skills is important. When you bolster his pride, you also bolster his belief in his own skills and in the worth of his healthy efforts.

Our goal is not only a learning child, but one who enjoys learning and feels able to learn. A baby's intellectual development is much entwined with his feelings. Whether or not he ever develops his full intellectual potential will depend on three things: the opportunity to do those activities that promote intellectual development, the confidence that he can do them if he tries, and the conviction that it's worth doing them. This is why it's so important that you show warmth, love and pride in your child's behavior and achievements without at the same time demanding success. Your encouragement should be for his attempts and should not be limited to only his successes. Encourage his efforts so he learns how much you value them. Such encouragement is not the same as "fussing over" him and interfering with his free play and self-direct actions. As in everything else, use your common sense and don't overdo.

The first game takes advantage of your baby's small muscle skill, his ability to crawl and move around, and his attraction to toys. The floor is the best place for this game.

Take one of his favorite toys and place it on a soft piece of material that he can grab and pull. Place both the toy and the material slightly out of reach. When he reaches for the material tell him what he's doing, "See, you're pulling on the blanket. Pull it to you and you can get the toy."

Demonstrate it for him if necessary.

Then say, "Let's try again. You get it now."

Be sure the toy is one he can get only by pulling the soft material to him. It should not be able to roll.

If he starts to play with it when he gets it, let him. Come back to the game a little later. Sometime parents have a tendency to teach too hard. They try to stay with something, or force the child to attend to an activity to suit them rather than the child.

Remember, we want him to learn how to get something by using another piece of material. He learns it best if he gets what he's after. Don't get so hung up in the "rules of the game" that you forget the child is the learner.

Bait Casting

Children love to pull on strings. You may remember the earlier game of grabbing and pulling on the elastic. Here we take advantage of his interest and skill to teach him a new way of getting something he wants. You can spread out this game over several weeks. The best arrangement is to sit at a table with your baby on your lap and place a piece of twine, shoestring, or cord on the table so he'll pick it up and pull on it.

Later, tie something interesting to one end of the string and put it at the far end of the table so the baby can get it by pulling the string to him.

When he has enjoyed this for a while, leave that string with the object tied to it and add two plain strings. Let him see what happens as he pulls each string. He will discover that only one string brings an object. Accompany this with words like "You didn't get anything," "Oh! that one got the toy."

After this general play, see if you can teach him always to pull the right string. Place them in different places where he can see the connection between string and toy and say, "Get the toy." This can be done on the floor, in a high chair, or wherever it is convenient. At this time he'll need to be able to see string and toy. Later games will be more like hide and seek.

First he'll be interested only in the string, then in the toy. Gradually he'll be aware of both, but he won't realize they are connected. Then he'll "experiment" and finally use the string to bring the toy to him.

Hide-and-Seek

The following three activities and some later ones are hide-and-seek games. They use your child's new ability to get around and to do things with his hands, and they're designed to teach him more about how the world works.

For the very young child, below six months of age, out of sight is out of mind. Now he's ready to learn that things exist even when he can't see them. This knowledge will add to his understanding that the world has some consistency, some dependability and some order to it — a conviction that's basic to intellectual development. Such facts about the world — that objects persevere, that they have a location in space, that you will *feel* them when you put your hand where you *see* them — all may sound like "second nature", but the truth is we weren't born knowing these things. We learn them. Every normal person learns them eventually, but the critical thing is *when* he learns them. Notice that these facts are not dead-end data like the date of Lincoln's birth or the capital of Albania. Instead, they're principles that, once grasped, enable the child to leap on to new clusters of knowledge whose explanation depends on these first principles. These first general rules about how things work are like portals to vast areas of knowledge. Of course, there will be other portals later on, but the longer the delay in getting through these first ones, the later everything else comes after.

Your job isn't one of forcing your baby *through* the portal, but it is one of bringing him *to* the portal so that, as early as he can, he'll be able to go through it on his own.

Begin with a simple game using a toy and some soft covering material, such as a blanket. Attract his attention to the toy and then partly hide it under the blanket so the baby can still see a part of it.

Then say, "Where did it go?" "Find the toy."

If he's puzzled and doesn't seem to know how to retrieve it, show him how. If he ignores the toy after it is hidden, play with it by yourself in front of him, but don't demand his attention or any action. He will, on his own, get interested in what you are doing.

Partly hide it again until he's able to get it himself.

Play the same game, but hide the toy completely under the soft material so he can see that something is under the blanket. Encourage him to lift it up and get his toy.

Repeat this for fun a number of times and then leave the child with both toy and blanket.

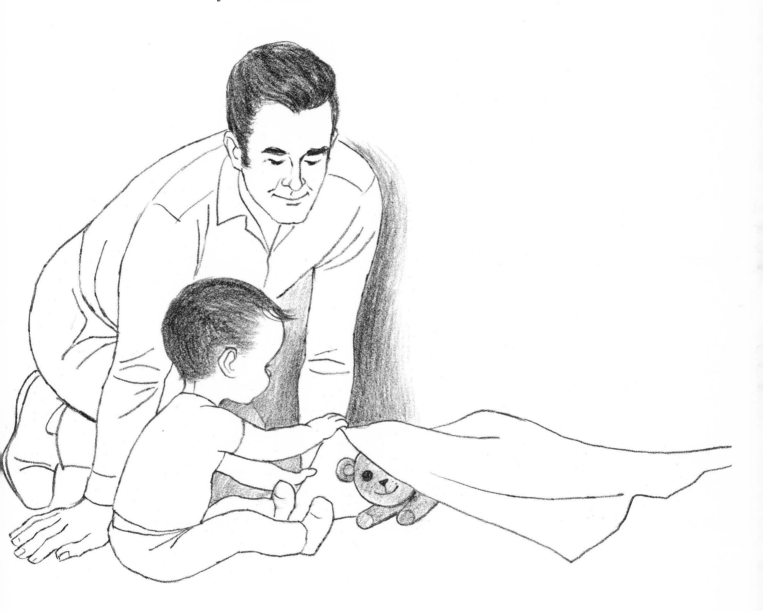

A more difficult hide-and-seek game is: Place a toy where the baby can see it and then put a blank piece of cardboard larger than the toy in front of it, blocking it. Be sure that the cardboard is blank and is not more interesting to the child than the toy.

His first efforts at getting the toy may be by knocking the card down. He is more likely to try a direct approach than going around the screen. Let him do it.

Then, show him how he can reach around the cardboard to get the toy. The first few times you do this he may not know or understand that the toy is still there. Pull the cardboard back and forth so he can see that the toy has not moved.

Be careful *not* to do this in a teasing way. Make it fun. If it's upsetting to him, drop it, let him have his toy. It will gradually become a game when he understands that the toy is still there and that he can get it by working at it.

A third approach to hide-and-seek is to place one of his favorite objects in a box or other container where he can no longer see it. Be sure the container is easy to open. Ask him, "Can you find it?" "Let's look in the box." "There it is!" "Can you get it now?"

The difference between this game and the blanket one is that there's nothing about the shape of the container to give away the fact that something's inside. He also has to work harder to get it.

Remember, don't tease, don't frustrate and don't force. Watch for the child "turning off."

When he discovers the toy's in the container, he'll enjoy putting it in, closing the box, opening it up, taking it out, and then he can be left to repeat this for his own continued learning and amusement.

Dialogue—2

Our first game had to do with sounds. Now that your child is older than six or seven months, we can come back to sounds in a somewhat different way. By now he's making a number of sounds that are used in our language. Most of his language learning is *not* the result of direct teaching of words but comes about because you have constantly been using words in sentences when you're with him.

In this activity we can take advantage of his desire to imitate what he sees and hears. Hold him face-to-face and make such sounds as: pa, ma, fa, da, ba, which are sounds he's been making randomly on his own. These are the easiest for him to make, and he'll soon begin to imitate you. When he does, laugh and smile and give him a squeeze and let him know you think it's fun. Keep the conversation going.

The difference between this game and the first one in the book is that now you are selecting from his *speech* sounds and getting him to imitate you. At three months, he was making *any* sound and you were imitating him.

Remember, this isn't all there is to language learning. The game simply encourages the expression of sound. He learns most about language from being surrounded by it at home. He'll show what language he knows by the way he responds to your words, his "hidden" vocabulary revealing itself in actions long before he speaks.

Man in Space

Your baby's increasing physical dexterity makes him ready for a new set of games that will promote his sense of space relations. Since he's able to connect eye and hand activities, you can try varieties of stacking and other space games.

Get three different-sized cans or plastic nesting jars or cubes that can fit loosely inside one another. They can be used both to build pyramids and to nest.

Start by building a pyramid. Sit on the floor next to the baby and place the three objects one on top of the other telling the baby what you are doing, "See, this one goes here, this one goes here."

Then encourage him to try, "Now you do it." Don't insist that he try to stack them in any order, for instance biggest on the bottom. Let him try it any way, but describe for him what is happening, why it works or why it won't. Your explaining without his trying wouldn't make any sense to him because almost any explanation would assume some things that seem so obvious that we must be born knowing them, when in fact they have to be learned — for example, that big things can't fit inside small things.

Show him again, when his facial expression or sounds suggest he's ready. Join in his glee when he gets them stacked up.

Turn the game into build-up knock-down, so that you and he stack and unstack and develop a cycle. Although he will not understand this now, practice in doing and undoing leads to the development of thoughtful problem solving behavior, which you can see in the early years of public school.

When he's had lots of fun stacking, change the game to nesting. You don't have to tell him when the objects don't nest; he can see it. This kind of game is self-correcting. When the smallest jar is placed inside the biggest, he discovers he can't put the middle-sized jar in place. Tell him what's happening, "Oops, it won't go, something's blocking it, try again."

Besides teaching about space relations, these games increase a child's sense of his ability "to do."

Rhythm and Finger Play

A child about nine months of age enjoys face-to-face rhythm games and finger play that you and he play together. They increase his language and they pay off in motor development. Remember you shouldn't expect the child to learn to count even though we're using counting games. You simply want to expose him to the rhythm and the order.

Use other songs that may have been handed down in your family and that carry on whatever may be special in your culture. Many of these songs are available on records, but the child's first experiences' with them are best when they are with you. He can enjoy the records for practice and repetition, but the interpersonal tie of mother, father and child is the best and most enjoyable way to learn.

He'll enjoy the activity and may want to continue after you are bored. If at all possible, let him set the pace. Remember it's his learning that is the aim.

Pat-a-Cake; This Little Pig; Here Is the Beehive; One, Two, Buckle My Shoe; Hickory, Dickory, Dock; and Row, Row, Row Your Boat are some sample rhythm games.

Row, Row, Row Your Boat
Row, row, row your boat,
Gently down the stream.
Merrily, Merrily, Merrily, Merrily,
Life is but a dream!

Here Is the Beehive
Here is the beehive. Where are the bees?
Hidden away where nobody sees.
Soon they come creeping out of the hive —
One! — two! — three! — four! — five!

Pat-a-Cake

Pat-a-cake, pat-a-cake,
    Baker's man!
Bake me a cake,
    As fast as you can.
Pat it, and turn it,
    And mark it with T,
Put it in the oven
    For Tommy and me!

Hickory, Dickory, Dock

Hickory, dickory, dock!
The mouse ran up the clock.
The clock struck one, and down he run.
Hickory, dickory, dock!

This Little Pig

This little pig went to market;
This little pig stayed home;
This little pig had roast beef;
This little pig had none;
This little pig said, "Wee, wee, wee!"
All the way home.

One, Two, Buckle My Shoe

One, two,
Buckle my shoe;
Three, four,
Shut the door;
Five, six,
Pick up sticks;
Seven, eight,
Lay them straight;
Nine, ten,
A big, fat hen.

GAMES FOR THE CREEPER-CRAWLER

The next series of activities are designed for babies between approximately eight months and thirteen months of age. You can use them in any order, but the earlier ones are usually simpler and easier. Your child will let you know by his interest, skill and the length of time he stays with something, whether the game is fun for him. If it is fun, this means it's teaching him because children learn primarily through games and activities. Things are fun to him when they are new, tick off his curiosity, fit in with what he can do, and push forward his present skill. He also enjoys going back sometimes, to familiar things. Let him have a mix of new and old.

The main purposes of the games for this period are to increase his small muscle skill in accomplishing things, further develop his language, increase his belief in his own ability, and continue the growth of his understanding that the world is an orderly, consistent place.

He'll now be able to follow simple commands, respond to gestures and wave bye-bye, and toward the end of this period he'll respond to familiar words in ways that show he understands them even though he doesn't say them. Sometime during this period he may become a standing child and perhaps even a walker, but all during this period he can get around under his own power.

"Getting around" means you have to be careful about what is around for him to handle. You've encouraged his curiosity, his desire to explore and reach and try. Now don't cut this off with lot's of "no," "don't touch," and mild slaps or other signals which tell him that he can't touch. He is too young yet to understand why some things are special or precious or even dangerous. Although it may be a bother, try to remove those things from his reach and store them away for the next few months until he can understand the difference. Get safety plugs for wall sockets.

You're not engaged in a contest of wills with your child. The wise teacher removes temptation so the child can freely explore without danger. He will still need to learn "no" where it's necessary, but he'll learn it in ways that won't curtail his desire to learn or explore.

Fetch

Let him use his new-found crawling skill to get something. The floor again is the best place.

Take a ball or anything that rolls and when you have the child's attention, roll it out of his reach; then say, "Go get the ball; bring it to daddy." Encourage him as he crawls toward it and brings it to you. Then roll it again. He'll enjoy both the motion and his ability to play with you. He may even try to roll the ball to you. If he does, the game may end up as a primitive form of catch. Most likely he'll simply carry it to you. Be prepared to change what you're doing to fit what he does after you get started.

The "fetch" game can be used throughout the day as you go about your household chores and baby crawls after you. In each room where you work there are lots of things he can carry. He can fetch a towel, a washcloth, a pan, part of a vacuum cleaner, if you place them where he can get them. When he sees that you do something with them after he brings them, he will begin to see that the fetching is useful. This increases the pay-off for you because now, for the first time, what he does helps.

From now on, you need to think of ways he can be a helper, even though from your point of view his help makes the job take longer. Remember you will need to "baby proof" the house. Remove from his reach the things you *don't* want him to get.

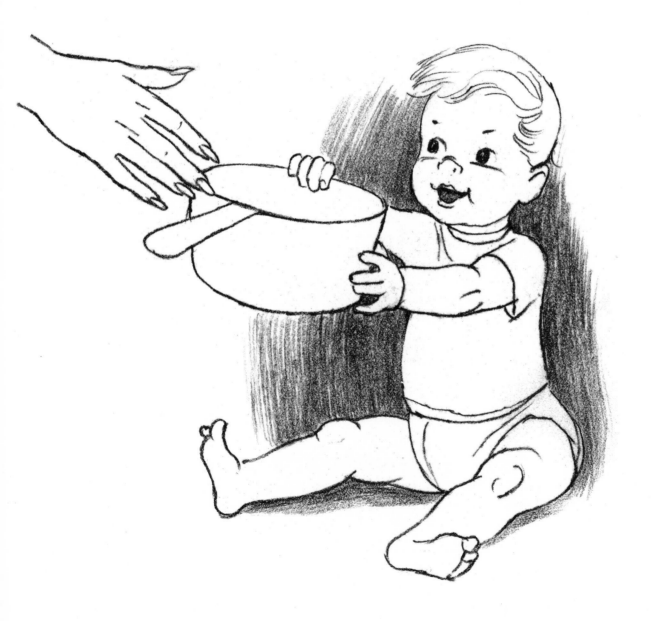

46

Fill 'er Up

Another "space" game that children enjoy, and which stretches their minds, is putting things into a jar or box and then emptying them out again.

You can start by putting a container and several objects in front of the baby, showing him how to fill it up (talking to him all the while about what you're doing), then turning it upside down to empty it. Once he's seen it, he can be on his own. Leave the container and objects around for free play, but make sure that none of the objects has a dangerous edge, or is small enough to be easily swallowed, or would be dangerous if tasted.

You'll be surprised how much time the baby can spend filling and emptying. Children have much longer attention spans for such games than we do. They need to have lots of time to repeat.

You may hear your child begin to talk to himself about what he's doing. He may use single words such as "fill" or, if the task doesn't work, "no". Talking to himself is one of the ways a child develops language and increases his understanding and control of behavior.

Searching Games

Searching games are great fun for a small child, and they're helpful, too. They allow him to use his new-found skills for getting around and exploring things, and they confirm his growing sense of consistency because he finds what he seeks where he expects.

The first of the hide-and-seek games in this set is complicated because the baby has to get past two barriers to find his object. You can use a container and the blanket, or a box inside of a box, or any system that calls on him to open two things to solve the problem of the missing toy.

First, let him see what you are doing. That is, place it inside the container while he watches. Show him how to find it. Then, hide the object and let him find it on his own.

Later on he may be able to change roles with you so that he hides and you find. Wherever possible in these games, see if you can change places with him.

Remember the language envelope! Talk with him about what you're doing.

This hide-and-seek game takes advantage of his increasing control of hands and fingers.

Wrap his favorite toy in a bag or piece of paper so it takes a little work for him to open it.

Ask him to get the toy from inside the package. He may just rip the paper. Don't discourage this but try again and show him how he can use his fingers to open it without destroying the paper.

When he's mastered this, you can step up the complications by using a rubber band to fasten the paper. After a little while he may be able to both hide and find his toy.

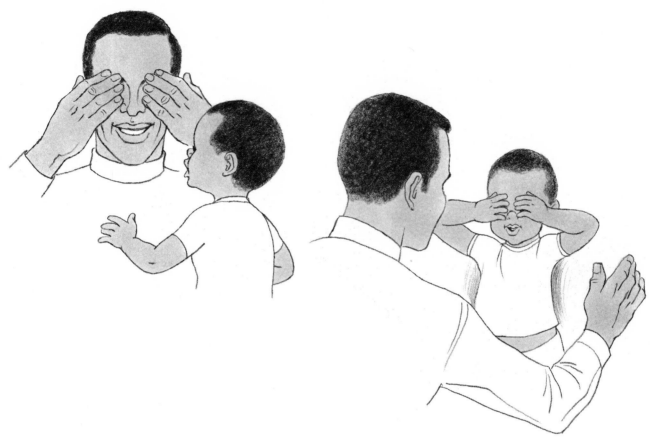

Peek-a-Boo

Up to now, you've used only objects in hide-and-seek games. Now your baby is ready to enjoy playing hide-and-seek with people. By this time, he knows that mother and dad come and go, but he knows he can count on seeing them again. However, he's at the interesting time when he thinks that if he can't see you, you can't see him. Peek-a-boo uses both his knowledge and lack of knowledge, his ability and desire to imitate.

Face the baby and cover your eyes and say, "Where did Johnny go? I can't see you." Then have him cover his eyes, and you should say, "Where did mommy (daddy) go? Johnny can't see me?" Then move into "Peek-a-boo, I see you."

Hide-and-Seek Me!

An extension of peek-a-boo is the regular game of hide-and-seek in which your whole body goes out of his sight and baby has to hunt in several places until he can find you.

You may want to start this as we did with the first hide-and-seek game by leaving some part of you visible, such as an arm or leg.

Try to make this a sharing game in which baby hides from you so that you take turns in hiding and seeking.

Robert Spaulding, a fellow psychologist, suggested this form of hide and seek, invented by his child. The child stood in back of the couch, holding on, and used knee-bends to duck out of sight. Up and down he went, in this very active version of peek-a-boo!

More Baby Power

The next two games combine the child's muscular ability, his developing sense of the fact that objects don't disappear because they can't be seen, and his ability to respond to simple commands. They challenge him and increase not only his problem solving skill but also his sense of ability.

Take a small container, such as an empty coffee can, and make a large enough slot in the plastic top. Fix the container so that the child can easily open it to get at its contents. It should not require any ability to screw or unscrew.

Take a pile of pennies, buttons or tokens and have him watch you as you drop these in the jar through the slot.

Let him help you empty the jar and then say, "Now you fill it. See if you can get these to go in."

When he's done it with you a few times, you can leave him with the container and the tokens to practice and repeat.

He may do it faster and faster, may try it with either hand; he'll invent a variety of his own ways for getting the tokens in and out of the can.

If you're watching, describe his activities out loud. It's not necessary to stay around. He can amuse himself for a long period of time.

A still more difficult form of hide-and-seek, because it requires more work and skill on the baby's part, is to place an object inside a matchbox and help him learn how to slide the box to get it out. Show and tell the baby what you're doing, "You have to push in here and it slides open." Close it.

When he can do this say, "Now you hide it and let me try to get it."

When he's enjoying the hiding and finding, you can leave him alone to do it. He'll pull it out and back, in and out, and practice his skill in using his hands to get at what he wants.

Remember that repetitive play for a child is a major way he learns.

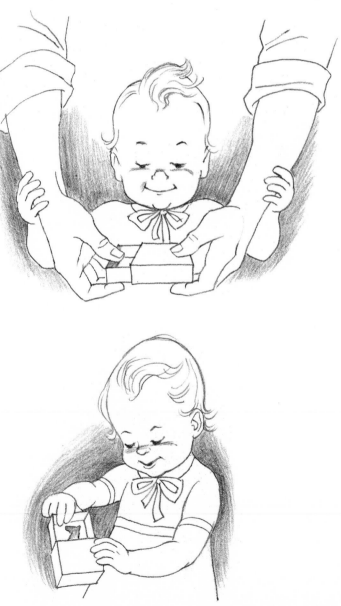

Blocks

Since your child can now handle small objects with his fingers rather well, he's ready for block play. Blocks are perhaps the best of all possible toys because he can do so many things with them. Start him out with just a few.

Place two blocks in front of him while you're both sitting on the floor and show him how one can be put on top of the other. Let him do it. Then add a third so he can build a simple three-block tower. Don't worry if they're not directly one on top of the other. This is a self-correcting activity. If he doesn't build well enough, it will just tumble down. He will enjoy the tumbling as much as the building.

56

A variation of this is to show him how you can place two or three blocks in a line on the floor and push them around. If he pushes on the third one, the first two will go straight for a few seconds and then get out of line. He'll enjoy watching this happen, and gradually he'll gain the skill needed both to build the tower straight and keep the blocks in line.

Leave his blocks handy. Add other blocks when you see he can build more and more. Don't criticize if it doesn't look like anything to you, or if his towers don't stand up. You don't need an elaborate set; pieces of two-by-four or two-by-two, sanded and smooth, work fine as beginning blocks. Toy stores offer many already packaged materials, but at this age fancy colors or alphabet letters aren't necessary. Plain old wood will do. Later on, more elaborate blocks can be useful.

The Supermarket School

Observations of young children placed in supermarket carts show interesting patterns of the way parents handle their children. Some parents take advantage of the time to keep language exchange and other learning experiences going. Others are continually disciplining and stopping their children from exploring this interesting world. The supermarket is a marvelous place, and children can learn many things. Your child is now about a year old and you can begin to use the supermarket as a school. You can use it in many ways for a long time.

As you go down the aisle with the child in the cart jump seat, have him help you put things in the cart. Call the objects by name, and give him some other fact about them. "Here's a red can of tomatoes. Let's put this in. Oh, here's a box of Cheerios. See the Cheerios on the cover? Let's put this in the cart. Here's some fresh lettuce. Oh, it's still wet. Let's put this in the cart."

Point out color, size, shape, texture. Show him that pictures tell what's inside.

Make a helper of him when you can. Use his need for activity, his desire to reach, grab and hold. It will take patience, but it produces far better results than the continual attempts to deny his basic urges for activity and curiosity.

If you can, let him see what happens to the things from the supermarket when you get home. Show him, with fresh fruits and vegetables, how the celery, lettuce, carrots he placed in the cart are cut, sliced, or peeled. Show him that what's on the outside label matches what's inside. Help him connect the picture with the object.

Do this as you do your regular unpacking and food preparation. It doesn't need a special time or place. Take advantage of the normal things in your day. The home is a 24 hour school for your child. There are no bells or periods, or separate subjects!

59

When he's older, he can help unload at home, and you can have him help sort cans, boxes, vegetables into piles and even put some away so he can see the order—these are cans and they go here; these are fresh things—they go into the refrigerator; these are boxes—they go here.

Further activities can be built around his pointing objects out on the store shelf for you to get. Children very soon know their favorite cereals by box, and recognize soft drinks and brands they've seen on T.V. He can point out to you where the cereals and soft drinks are, and check to be sure you've picked the right ones. This will probably be some time between age two and three, but these early experiences build toward that time.

The truth is that your child has things to learn everywhere he goes—not just at home, not just at home and the store. The street, the park, a ride in the car—everything offers opportunities to increase his awareness of what's around him and to see ties between familiar things and new things. Talk to him when you're riding or walking together; point things out; exclaim at new and exciting things; convey the fun of discovery.

Remember: Almost any remarks or explanations, even if he can't really understand them, are better than silence. The one word of caution is that you mustn't expect him to be caught up by all the things you are. If something of interest to you—like, say, an historical monument—is too strange and removed for him, he won't pay attention, he won't listen, and there's no point trying to force his attention. Take your cues from his behavior. He'll let you know when things are interesting.

61

ACTIVITIES FOR THE STANDER AND TODDLER

Some time between 11 and 19 months (of course it may be somewhat earlier or later) your child will pull himself up to stand, begin climbing up and down, stand and walk alone. He'll move from a four-legged to a two-legged creature. This increases his range of activities tremendously and offers many opportunities for new activities and games to play. During this first part of toddlerhood he will enjoy just using his new-found skill and will want to climb up and down and walk around for the pure pleasure of the exercise. Toward the end of the toddler period he'll use these new skills to do things. He'll want to climb to get some place, like the kitchen shelf for the cookie jar, walk to some place, such as a tot lot. He'll enjoy various round and circle type games and the pleasure of going for walks.

This is a critical time for language learning. Continual exchange between you and the child is vital, but remember that he doesn't learn language from direct teaching or simple imitation. He will learn some vocabulary this way, but he learns the pattern of language from hearing his parents and family members accompany their words with gestures and feelings in action situations.

He's ready now for the activity known as "sorting". He's already learned to sort some of the things around him. During this period he will make much more progress in his ability to group familiar objects as he uses and plays with them.

62

Knock the Bunny Off—
An Action Game for Father and Child

This game is recommended for fathers because of the amount of exertion involved. It can provide exercise for both members of the family as well as developing the important relationship that children must have with father. Throughout these activities we've usually spoken of the parent as mother and the child as he. But it could be father and daughter just as well.

When the child can stand up by holding on, place him in a play-pen or other large area that provides him with moving space but also a hand-hold. Take a favorite toy (such as bunny rabbit or teddy bear) and place it on a corner of the play-pen where it can stand alone. Encourage the child to use one of his hands to knock it off outside the area while he's holding on with the other.

Father's big job is to stoop and retrieve and place it on some other point so that the child has to move around to continue the game. He will enjoy his movement, the fun of knocking something down, and the delight of seeing father at work. This can be accompanied with lots of laughing and words. The only problem is the child can last longer than the father. I know—my son invented the game!

If . . . Then

By now your baby has had lots of experience placing objects in containers. He's had an open jar and then a jar with a slot.

Now introduce a screw type jar. Show him how to screw it on and off and give him some objects to place in it. After he gets the idea, let him do it alone.

This play gives the child a chance to practice not only the use of his hands to manipulate the jar lid, but also in seeing the orderly sequence of in and out, in and out, on and off, on and off. This sequence later becomes basic to his thought in handling objects in the primary grades and to hypothesis-making in early adolescence. It's a primitive beginning of "If I do this, then that will happen."

Who Do You Know?

The child will now be ready for and enjoy more language play—although, of course, you've been using words in connection with every game. Now he has a basic knowledge that mommy and daddy and he and other family members look different and sound different. Here's a game for when several family members are together. Say, "Where is daddy?" Point to daddy. "Who's that?" while someone points to mommy. "Where is Johnny?" Point to Johnny.

After pointing to various family members, who should respond with smiling and saying, "Yes, I'm _____," you can now have him go to the person.

A more difficult form of "Who Do You Know" is to tell people by voice. This puts peek-a-boo or hide-and-seek together with names of family members. Have him cover his eyes and have someone talk and say, "Who was that? Go to who was talking." This may be much too hard immediately but can be kept in reserve for when you and your baby will enjoy it.

Reading Readiness

Your baby will like a lot of action and movement. The block play, peek-a-boo, crawling, playing with the containers and objects are just right. He'll also begin to appreciate some sit down, quiet time, especially before naps or bedtime. He needs some tapering off between high levels of activity and periods of rest.

This is a good time to introduce the beginnings of reading-type play. This doesn't mean you're trying to teach the child to read in any formal way. The play is designed to make the child aware of reading materials, and to tie together your reading and his interest in what you do.

Take one of your magazines, preferably one with many pictures (and one with which you are finished) and ask him to sit on your lap to read with you. Show him how to turn the pages and let him look at it in any way he wants to—right side up, upside down, right to left, left to right, turning several pages together or one at a time. Let him take the magazine to bed with him and don't be disturbed if it is torn.

The second stage is to sit with him and point out some pictures in the magazine.

To prepare for this, find pictures that you know are repeated like a man or a car, a dog, or cat, or other objects he's seen in real life and with which he is familiar. You may want to mark the pages in some fashion so that you can get to them rapidly.

Speak to him in sentences such as "See, there's a car" or "Look, that car's like ours." "There's a man. Is that daddy?" The child will usually respond in single words which may not be as clear as yours: "cah" "doggie." When he does, say, "Good, that's right; that's a car."

After this, let him fool with the magazine in his own fashion. Let it be his. If he doesn't wreck it too badly, use the same magazine again. He will enjoy it even more as he becomes familiar with it. And he will *see* it better, especially if there are complicated pictures in which he can spy out more and more details.

Start with just one or two things. Don't overload with too many things for him to name. If he points on his own to something and gives it a name (or close to it!), pick it up and use it. Take advantage of any of his words and activities and gradually let him do most of the pointing and naming.

Sorting

By now, he's had a variety of experience in dealing with objects of different sizes and shapes, things that feel different in his hand and look different. He knows some things by name, and he has built in his mind some crude groups of things that are pushable, climbable, eatable, holdable.

These next few games will give him some more experience in simple grouping. They are free-play activities. He should be allowed to do with the materials whatever he wishes and to discover, through dealing with them, that some objects are alike and go together.

Look around the house and select any two sets of objects

such as empty soft drink cans (be sure there are no sharp edges) and some wooden blocks—about four of each object is plenty.

He'll most likely discover that not only can both be stacked, and perhaps even mixed, but that they make a different sound, the cans can roll, he can put things in the cans but not in the blocks. It's all part of his expanding education about how the world and the things in it work.

If you want to see if he has some idea about grouping, place a can in one spot and a block in another. Ask him, "Put all the cans like this over here," as you point to both a can and the spot. Don't be surprised if he can't do it. He may not understand such words as "like this."

If you wish to teach this more directly after he has had much free play, show him by your demonstration how all the cans go together and all the blocks go together.

Accompany your actions by words, "See, this is a can. It's cool and it's round and it makes this kind of sound. It goes over here. Here is another one just like it. It's cool and round and it makes the same sound. It goes over here."

Since this is a new experience, it is best to move slowly. Keep this free play and discovery as much as possible.

Another play activity may be done with blocks of different shapes. Put out some squares, rectangles and triangles (don't worry about teaching these words) and let him do what he wants with them. He may simply bang them, pile them, push them, stack them.

This is a first experience with blocks of different shapes so don't try and teach too much. Let him enjoy handling, seeing and using. Later on he'll make use of these more purposefully, and still later he'll learn the correct labels.

Let your child help you sort the laundry. "These are daddy's clothes; these are mommie's clothes; these are your clothes."

The idea behind this is not that the child will always sort correctly, or have any great skill in helping, but that he will see that categories are used in daily activities, and are helpful. Later on, he can group by type and color.

Words In Action

Vocabulary develops when actions and words are brought together.

In the kitchen have your child help you in regular household chores. Ask him to hand you the dish towel, get a paper towel, dry a (preferably nonbreakable) dish, fold the towel, put it away, turn the faucet on, turn the faucet off, find out which one's hot, find out which one's cold, get a pot, get a pan, and the like.

He'll learn the words for common household materials through seeing how they're used and using them rather than being presented with a quiz game of naming.

Water Play

Children this age love to handle a variety of materials and see what happens to them. As one noted authority (Gardner Murphy) said, "Children need time for messing and manipulating."

Water play lets a child learn how liquids behave and how they look in different sized containers. For several years to come the child will be fooled by the capacity of different-shaped containers; for example, he will tend to think that a tall thin glass must have more water in it than a short fat one. Right now you're simply providing him with some of the experiences that will eventually help him to grasp the facts about such things as varying volumes.

Take two or three containers of different sizes and fill the smallest with water. Let your child watch you pour it into the second sized container, then the largest one, and then back into the first. When he reaches to imitate you, let him pour the water back and forth.

Be sure that you prepare for this by placing some protective material around so that you don't spend your energy worrying about the spills which are bound to come!

Describe for him what he's doing. For example, "Now you're pouring it from a big one into a little one. Watch the water pour. Now that cup is empty. Pour it back the other way. See how it fills up."

A variation and enlargement of this activity for outdoor use is the sandpile in which he can use different size cups. Later on he can use a shovel to fill his containers. He will also like his first equation, sand + water = mud.

Action Songs

By now your baby will have developed some sense of time. He knows that when certain routine things happen he can expect something to follow. For example, he knows that being placed in his high chair (or wherever he usually eats) means it's meal time. When he sees you putting on your coat he may go to the door.

There are a number of songs and rhyme games that combine his need for activity and his ability to stand and walk, and which develop awareness that one action precedes another. Some samples:

Pop Goes the Weasel

All around the carpenter's bench
The monkey chased the weasel,
The monkey thought twas all in fun,
Then POP, goes the weasel.

Ring Around the Rosie

Ring around the rosie
A pocket full of posie
Ashes, ashes;
All fall down!

London Bridge Is Falling Down

London Bridge is falling down
  falling down, falling down
London Bridge is falling down,
  my fair lady

An added advantage to these round games is that other children can participate. The activities described up till now have all been for you and one child. Rhythm and rhyme games permit him to begin his experience with other children in a social setting.

ACTIVITIES FOR THE OLDER TODDLER

The child between about 17 months and two years is an active, energetic, curious, loud individual. He wants to get into things,to explore. He loves to use his new-found skill in walking on his own.

During this period he will make great strides in language development. By the age of two—or within a few months after— he can name a number of objects, ask for things with words, use simple two-word sentences and arrive at that first verbal sign of his sense of identity, the use of "me." He'll advance from using his own name in talking about himself—"Danny fall down"—to saying, "Me fall down."

Your behavior is very important as he explores his world and uses his new-found language to express himself and to ask for things. You should encourage him, talk to him a good deal, give him reasons for what you do and what you ask him to do, and, most important of all, *listen* to him.

Your behavior toward his actions should also change a bit. What he needs now is a mixture of time with you and time by himself to conduct his own play. Earlier you had to place most of the objects within his reach, and start many of the activities, even though hopefully you took your cue from his own ways of playing. But now more and more he'll engage—and needs to en-gage—in free play in which he knows you are encouraging him, are there when he needs you, and are enjoying his inventions and discoveries, but in which he's running things.

In some games, he'll invent the game and involve you. Ob-viously we can't present such games in the book because they belong to the child, but don't hesitate to join him in play when he wants you to.

During these six months or so he'll get better with the blocks and enjoy them more; he'll be able to arrange objects in groups; and he'll put together simple jigsaw puzzles. All of these are important steps in his intellectual development.

The Old Shell Game

With all his experience at handling containers and succeeding in a variety of hide-and-seek games, he's now ready to enjoy this first introduction to the old shell game.

In this variation he has to notice that the size of the can is the important clue.

Take three cans of different sizes. Let him see you place a toy under one of the cans; then change the position of the cans by shuffling them around.

Ask him to guess which can. When he points to the wrong can, lift it and say, "No, not here! Try again! Where could it be?" When he points to the right can, join in his glee.

When he is pretty comfortable with guessing the right can after he has seen you put the object under it, ask him to close his eyes or turn around and not peek. Use the large can and hide the toy. Keep hiding it under the large can until he points right to it to find the object.

If you want, when he is skilled, you can mix him up by shifting to the smallest can for several times in a row. Don't make it too hard and don't tease.

Another way to play is to select three cans that contain things familiar to him because he can recognize the label. See if he can use the label as the important cue.

He may enjoy playing tricks on you. If he wishes, let him hide the object and see if you can guess it.

Your child has just played the shell game using shape and perhaps something about the label to help him win the game. Now he's ready to pay attention to location and arrangement. Learning this not only increases his knowledge of space relations but also gives him the necessary background for the ideas of number, order and measurement that come later on.

Take three cans or jars of different sizes. Let him see you place a toy under one of the cans and then shuffle them around.

If you placed the object under the can that was on his right, make sure that the can ends up there after shuffling. Now ask him to guess which can. Let him point to the top of the can, and if it's the wrong one, simply say, "no," and ask him to guess again until he guesses the right-hand can. Then let him look under it to see that the toy is there.

Repeat this several times until he's fairly confident and points immediately to the right-hand can. Then say, "Watch me. See where it goes now," and place it under the left-hand can. Repeat the shuffling and game until he consistently guesses the left-hand can. Be sure you are consistent and don't mix him up. Now have him cover his eyes.

He may want to play this with you, and he may be inconsistent. Don't expect that he will use location when he controls the cans.

You can begin to introduce the words, right and left and middle, but don't drill them or expect him to use them. Be careful that if you use them, you have a constant place, his right, his left. Don't shift back and forth between yours and his, because he looks at objects in a mirror way. If you want to check this out, raise your right hand the chances are that he will raise his left.

Guess Which Hand

Another form of the shell game is the hand guessing game.

Take a small object (small enough so that his fist would cover it), show it to the child and then shuffle it back and forth in your fists.

Show him both fists and ask him to guess which hand has the object.

If he points to the wrong hand, open it and say, "no, no, it's not here. Where could it be?" and close the hand again. When he points to the right hand, let him take what he finds and say, "Yes, that's right; you guessed it. Now let's try again."

After he seems to understand this, try saying "no" when he picks the wrong hand without opening your hand to see if he moves directly to the other hand. If not, let him open the "no" hand until he begins to understand that "no" means "try the other."

At the beginning, you may want to keep the object in the same hand, as you did in the Shell Game. Then make it more a game of chance.

This is not too easy a game. Be careful that it does not seem to the child to be teasing. If he gets tired or irritable, quit and come back to it some other time. If he seems to catch on and enjoy it, your next step up, a little later, will be to see if he can hide something in his hands for you to guess. This may not occur for another month or so.

Remember these aren't lessons; they should be fun for both of you. Try it, but drop it if the child doesn't seem to take to it. Don't push.

82

Quiet Time Language Activities

Use a child's picture book. Don't be concerned with the story. Let your baby point to pictures. When he does, describe the pictures and what the person is doing. He may enjoy the repetition of pointing to a particular type of picture again and again. For example, in animal picture books he may simply turn each page and say, "dog."

Use other magazines and books and objects around the house to connect the pictures in his picture book with the real object and with other pictures.

He may try to lift the object off the page because he still doesn't understand that pictures are not the real thing, but this is part of the fun of watching him grow.

Body Parts

Your child will now be interested in body parts. Sit him on your lap and ask him to feel your face; let him handle your ear, for example. As he does, say "That's my ear, now touch yours." Help him if he can't do it by himself. Then have him feel his own. He will discover that you have two ears, although he won't know the word "two." You can do this with eyes, nose, mouth, teeth, tongue, fingers, hair. The pattern is for him to explore yours; then find his. Accompany the actions with words that both name the parts and describe his behavior in touching them.

When he seems to have this pretty well down pat, try asking him to point out body parts for you. "Where is your tongue? Show me Johnny's ear. Where are your eyes?"

And What The Parts Do

There is a difference between naming a body part and understanding what it does. Children learn about such things best by action rather than words.

You played "peek-a-boo" earlier, so he's probably familiar with the fact that when he covers his eyes, he can't see. Ask him to stop you from seeing, and encourage him to place his hands over your eyes.

Then ask him to stop you from talking and encourage him to place his hand over your mouth.

Ask him if he can stop you from listening or hearing. This may be much harder because there's no outward way for him to know what the ears do. Try placing your hands gently over his ears and taking them away as a beginning step. Then move to your ears and make a back and forth game of this.

You can go on to other senses such as tasting and smelling when you feel that he's ready to try, enjoy, and learn these.

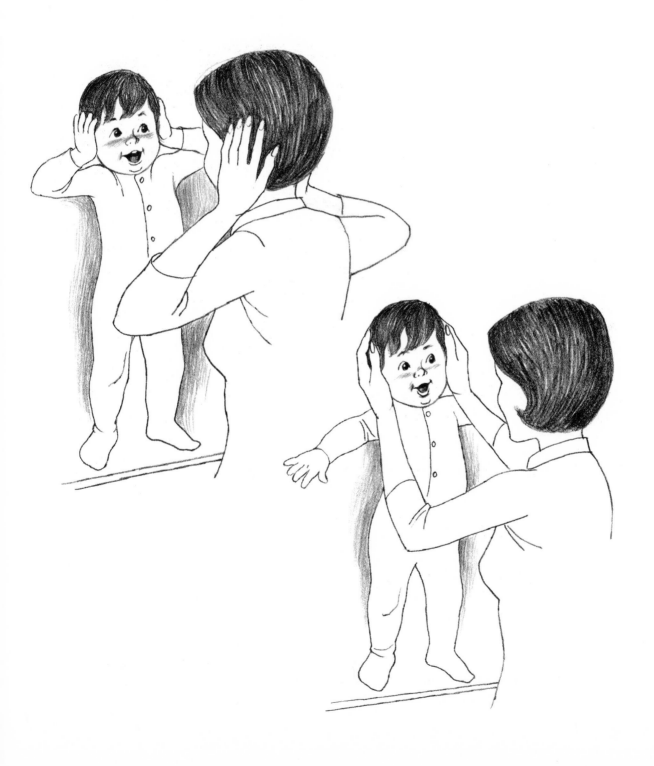

Some More Words in Action

Most children have a favorite stuffed animal or a doll. Have the child do different things with his animal—make it sit, make it stand, make it walk, lie down.

After he has engaged in a variety of actions with this animal, find other toys or objects that can be used in several ways. Help him learn to climb on and off a chair, push and pull a toy, run a car about the floor, carry objects from place to place. Our goal is vocabulary development; our idea is that words for things are learned through action with these things.

"It's a Bird, It's a Plane . . ."

The child is surrounded by many sounds, some of which have become quite familiar. Make a game out of imitating common sounds. When a jet goes overhead, say, "Listen, it goes zoom. Let's try and zoom." When a truck goes by, imitate its sound. Chirp like a bird; meow like a cat.

The best times to do this are when the child has just heard the real thing. Make the sounds yourself; then ask him to make it and, when he does, even if it doesn't sound very close, smile or laugh and repeat the sound.

You can match actions to sounds as an introduction to later dramatic play. If he's just seen a jet and imitated its noise, you may want to stretch your hands and have him stretch his and "become" a jet. If he knows the sound of cars and trucks and has some car and truck toys, you can push one of the toys and make the sound, and he'll soon be doing it too.

The One Piece Jigsaw Puzzle

Your child's experience with shape and space has been three-dimensional (blocks, containers). Now it's time to experiment with flat shapes. Take a piece of cardboard or construction paper and, beginning at the edge, cut out a square so that the missing piece can be slid directly into place.

Show him how the cut-out piece fits in and then have him try. Once he gets it in he'll enjoy sliding it in and out.

Do the same thing with a triangle.

Now make it a little harder. Cut the square out of the inside of the paper. He'll have to jiggle it around to get it to fit in, and this may take more practice. This will help him learn about size, boundary line, and position.

Now try this with the triangle.

You can use any variety of shapes, circles, semi-circles, but do them one at a time until he can easily fit the cut-out into the sheet.

You can then vary this puzzle by showing him the cut-out sheet for the square while leaving square, triangle, and circle shapes available for him to try until he gets square with square. Let him discover for himself the fact that it doesn't fit, rather than telling him "no" or stopping him from trying to place the wrong piece into the cut-out.

You can think of many different approaches to this first jigsaw puzzle. You can make a color puzzle, or one in which he has to match texture, such as pieces of cardboard or pieces of construction paper. Be inventive! (But stay with *one* cue at a time!)

Block Play

The next three games all use blocks to increase skill in sorting.

Set out six or eight blocks of two different sizes.

Let him play with them in any way he wants. He can build a tower, lean them against each other, make a road. After he has handled them for a while, take two of them, one of each size, and place one on top of the other.

Then ask him, by pointing to a particular block, to give you a little one, then a big one until you have used all the blocks to make something. You don't have to use them in any order, but be sure you call his attention to the differences in size.

Then let him play again with these blocks.

Using the same set of blocks, jumble them altogether in a pile, take one, and ask the child now to "Give me another one that's this size, or looks like this." Explain to him what "same size" means by running your hand and his around the edges, have him look, and turn at different angles.

When he hands you another block, let him compare the two by holding them together and matching edges. Ask again, "Is it just like this? Are these alike?" If he says "yes" put them together in the pile (even if it's wrong!).

Now take the other size block and do the same thing.

Continue this until all the blocks have been piled.

If he doesn't understand what you mean by "alike" or "just like this," perhaps there are other words he knows that you can use to get at the same idea. In any case, don't push. These are hard ideas for him. If he isn't having fun, let him move back to free play.

Try to have him place the two blocks together and handle them so that he gets through eyes and hands the idea of "sameness," even though he doesn't understand the words. This is where your creativity comes in, thinking of your own approaches.

Children of this age (and indeed many up to age four or five) can't *name* color although it's obvious that they recognize color differences. This game teaches your child to *use* color differences as a key in the same way that we wanted him to use size.

Give him two sets of blocks—some of them red, some of them blue. Don't use more than two colors to begin.

Let him play with the blocks in his usual way.

Then join him on the floor, pick a block and ask him to give you one that looks like it. From here on, the game is like the preceding one except color is the key.

If he seems to understand and enjoy doing this, you may want to add a third color.

Children this age pay attention to one fact about an object at a time. Later on, you might want to have him notice both shape and color or both size and color. For now, just stick to one thing at a time.

The name of the color is not important at this time. You should use the name red and blue, but he will not call them by name, nor will he hand you a block by color without more drill than it may be worth. There's time enough to learn the name of a color. Here we want him to use the fact of color.

He knows the names of things such as important people (mommy, daddy, Johnny) or objects (bottle, cup, spoon), but naming an object is quite different from using a word that describes it (big, round, red, fuzzy). Describing is far more difficult and shouldn't be expected of toddlers and run-a-bouts. Even though you've used these words and he may understand them because he can respond to them, he doesn't use them himself. Actions and the thoughts connected to them come ahead of words. Involve him in lots of actions that make use of size, shape, color, texture, function, and the words will come.

New Sorts of Sorts

The next three activities involve sorting by shape. You may want to use the Tupperware toy for these.

Empty the shaped, plastic blocks out of the toy by pulling on the handles. Let your child help you pull the toy apart and, as soon as he can, let him do it by himself.

While you hold the container, let him take one of the shapes and hunt for the right hole, using trial and error. Don't stop him from trying to place the shape in the wrong one. This is a self-correcting toy; he will soon discover it doesn't fit.

You can accompany his trials with language by explaining to him what is happening. "Oh, you're trying to get that one in there. It won't go. That's hard! It doesn't fit."

If he persists on a particular hole, suggest to him that he try another but don't solve the problem for him.

If he seems to pick it up pretty fast, fine. If after a while it seems too hard but he doesn't want to stop, turn the ball-shaped container so that you bring the correct hole into view. Then encourage him to try that spot. When it goes in, say, "Oh, fine. You got it! Good! Let's try another." Help him a few more times by turning the ball to bring the right hole into view. Don't make it too easy but give him this lift.

Don't make an issue about the names of the shapes. This is a matching game, not a naming game!

When he seems to have the hang of it, give him lots of free play with this toy. He'll pick up speed, and stay with the game for many minutes at a time.

By this age your child will enjoy taking turns with you if he's also active in the game. Taking turns doesn't mean he has to wait while you do something. Let him hold the ball and you hold the shape. Purposely try to put the shape in the wrong place and observe how he tries to help you.

He may either turn the ball, as you did, so that you can find the right shape, or he may hand you a new shape to fit the hole. In either case, follow his lead with excitement and enjoyment.

One boy with whom I played this game developed consider-able skill in looking at the shape in my hand, perhaps a foot to two feet away from him, and turning the ball so that the correct shape was on top. Then, he would nod at me and signal okay. To see at that distance that the three-dimensional shape is the right one for that hole is a high level of skill.

The Tupperware toy can also be used to increase the child's knowledge of order. He enjoys rhythm and has had some experience with rhymes, songs, and counting games, so this can be put together with the matching.

Hold the toy so he can see the shape that's on top. Ask him to find the one that goes in there from the pile. When he does and starts to put it in, have him give it to you. Hold it over the top of the hole and say, "Ready, set," and then have him hit it in as you say, "Go!" Before too long he'll be saying "Go!" as he hits it with you.

After using "ready, set, go," you may want to vary it with "One, two, three, go!"

After he's enjoyed this with you, you can retreat and leave him alone. You will hear "one, two, three, go!" following you around the house.

Catch

Another game which requires taking turns while staying active is the child's first game of catch. This, again, is suggested for dads. Sit on the floor with your legs apart and have him sit opposite you so that the soles of your feet touch. Get a ball that's not too big so that there's sufficient rolling space and roll it to him and have him roll it back to you. The repetition and rhythm and the fun of playing with dad can keep this game going for quite a while.

We are still stressing the language envelope. As you roll the ball back and forth, use such words as "rolling," "my turn," "your turn," "Johnny has it," "I have it," and also praise his performance, "That's a good roll!"

If by accident the ball gets outside the playing field of your legs, turn that into fun as you go to find it and sit back down again.

Gradually, you might increase the distance so that there is open space between you, and he can begin to correct his aim and improve his accuracy.

This can be a three-way or four-way game involving all members of the family. As he grows, it can shift from rolling to throwing on a bounce to regular catch.

The only trouble with this game is the adults will wear out long before the child.

Simple Jigsaw Puzzles

Your child is now familiar with parts of his body—from the games with the mirror, and touching and learning the names of parts of your face. He's looked at pictures of people and familiar things in magazines. He's had experiences in matching shapes both in three-dimension and on flat surfaces.

Now he's ready for simple jigsaw puzzles of objects and people. Scout the stores for well-made wooden or plastic puzzles that have only a few pieces. One may have several trucks, another may have several pieces of fruit, another may have people. These first puzzles should be the complete object to be placed into the shape of the object—that is, a truck into a cut-out shape of the truck.

These puzzles are self-teaching. Simply provide them for him and "kibitz." He won't be bored with doing the same puzzle many times and will probably develop a favorite one that he'll return to even after he can do more complicated ones.

When he is fairly skilled at this, try a simple puzzle that divides an object into its recognizable parts—that is, if it's a puzzle of a person, the eyes, the ears, the nose are separate pieces. Don't use puzzles that are cut so he can't rely on the combination of shape and something that's familiar.

He'll tell you by his behavior how soon he's ready to move on to more and more complicated puzzles.

Lots of Blocks

This is just a reminder that wooden blocks offer endless possibilities for creative and dramatic play. Increase the number of his blocks to a regular starter set. This would consist of about 48 blocks: squares, triangles, rectangles, arches, some cylinders, and half curves. A modular set is the best so that all of the pieces can fit together well. You may not want to put all the pieces out at once, but give him enough to try his hand at building, and increase the number as soon as he can use them.

Blocks are highly creative materials. Don't impose designs on him or make too many suggestions as to what he should build. Let him build both out and up as he wishes, and he will develop many interesting designs. He will also find out about the "laws of physics" through practical experience and direct contact. He will discover that there are some things you just can't do. He now may also enjoy alphabet blocks, or other cube shaped blocks with pictures on them. Let him discover the shapes, don't drill him on the alphabet!

Push-Pull

Children this age love to push and pull and carry. There are many push and pull toys available, most of which make noise. Since he'll play with it for many hours, find one that you can live with so that you don't discourage him from using it. If you think this is noise, wait till he's a teenager!

Make-Believe

At about the age of two, child's play takes an interesting turn. The child puts into use the many motor skills, activity patterns and observations he's made over the last two years. I mentioned earlier that skill learning goes through three stages. First, he gets the skill down pat, such as walking, rolling a ball, stacking a tower, matching a shape.

Second, he becomes fancier in using this skill: walking faster, rolling harder, matching shapes with both hands. During this second stage, the child sees how much he can stretch his skill. Older children do this when they're learning to ride a bike or play ball. They start with riding the right way, then standing up, then riding with one hand, then no hands. An outfielder practices catching with both hands, catching with one hand, turning around and catching the ball behind his back, waiting for the last minute to run to see if he can judge it properly. All of these are second stage activities, and they've been about as far as your child has gone.

Now, around two, he adds on the third stage. He uses his skill as a part of another game or another activity. Earlier when he was learning to creep and crawl, he repeatedly crept and crawled. In the second stage, he worked on speed until he gave it up and stood. In this third stage he may creep and crawl again, but this time it's in hide-and-seek or cowboys and Indians. It has a purpose. There are any number of "make-believe" games you can invent and play with your child. He'll also invent many on his own.

Hold a make-believe telephone conversation. Use either a real phone or a toy one, stand at a distance, and "talk."

Push two chairs together and turn it into make-believe car with the child as the driver. Tell him where you want to go and let him drive you there.

About playing house: Your child learns many things about you, and how you feel, through making believe he is you. This role-playing helps him sort out and understand the ways of other people. In this type of make-believe, your child can, through his play, make reality fit his view. When he is scolded for making a mess at a meal, he can become the scolder, and shake his finger at his pet toy dog, or he can be kind and "help" his dog clean up the mess. In either case, this type of make-believe aids the child in developing his view of himself, and of you.

Provide a place that can be "house," and allow the child to engage in this imaginative play. Don't intrude, and don't attempt to force "reality" into the situation.

Have him imagine that familiar objects can be used in make believe to be other things. A pencil can be a car, a block can be an airplane, a shoe box can be a hat. Fool around with using the common and familiar in new and different ways.

Make believe is important to the child. It's the way he gets a feel for how things are outside of him. He develops his sense of reality and his sense of self from this imaginative play. Encourage it, see it as learning, and don't be concerned that it isn't "true."

Many of the activities in this book have exposed him to parts of the real world and how it works. Many have been self-correcting in that he could see whether he was accomplishing something or not. Now, with that behind him, he needs to use imaginative play to deal with his feelings and get ready to move forward again.

Copying Dad or Mom

Your child is now ready to be a "helper" in the regular household chores. You've introduced him to helping in the "supermarket store" activities and in the kitchen and laundry. Now he can do far more, and, because he enjoys large muscle activities and getting around, he'll see chores as fun.

What does dad do around the house that offers opportunities? If you have a lawn, children can help in yard work. Regardless of where you live, there's garbage to be taken out, small items to be repaired, nails to hammer in, pictures to be hung, furniture to be moved.

What does mom do? There's at least laundry and cooking and cleaning. Try to think of what part of it can involve the child. He may not be able to do much, but it is important that he see you at work and shares in it any way he can.

If you share all the chores, it needn't make any difference if your child is a boy or a girl. A boy can learn that copying dad does not exclude helping mom. He can see that mom and dad help each other. He will build his picture of a family and his notion about male and female roles from this type of helping.

Roughhouse

Boys especially need active play with their fathers or with older brothers or other men. They'll enjoy body contact, climbing on you, wrestling, piggyback.

Although this looks purely physical, it contributes to ideas about being a boy.

Girls, too, enjoy some of this, and they need their fathers as models of male behavior, too.

Remember they're young and small and in wrestling you don't have to win. The idea isn't to show how strong you are, but to let them enjoy the vigorous activity.

Pencil Play

Toddlers can be scribblers. You may want to take advantage of this by providing some large sheets of paper and pencils or crayons. This should be a supervised activity, because the crayon or pencil may soon leave the paper and cover walls, floors and what-have-you.

By the time he is about two, he may be able to make a straight line somewhat like the one you can make for him.

He'll enjoy the sheer activity. Don't push for any "product." It's enough that he sees that what he does with his hand results in a mark on a paper.

When our children were young, my wife turned the refrigerator into an easel, and our children used finger paints to decorate it. The paint washes off easily, and the activity is great for learning and expressing.

Rocking the Boat

The toddler enjoys activities that provide a rocking and swaying motion in which he can control the speed and effect. Rocking chairs, rocking boats, horses, swings, all are most attractive to him.

Although it looks to you (and to him) as "just play," it's important to him and helps him learn to handle his body and see his effect on the things of his world. He's testing his body against the things around him and learning much about both. His method is play, very active play, without any concern for accomplishments, but the accomplishments are there.

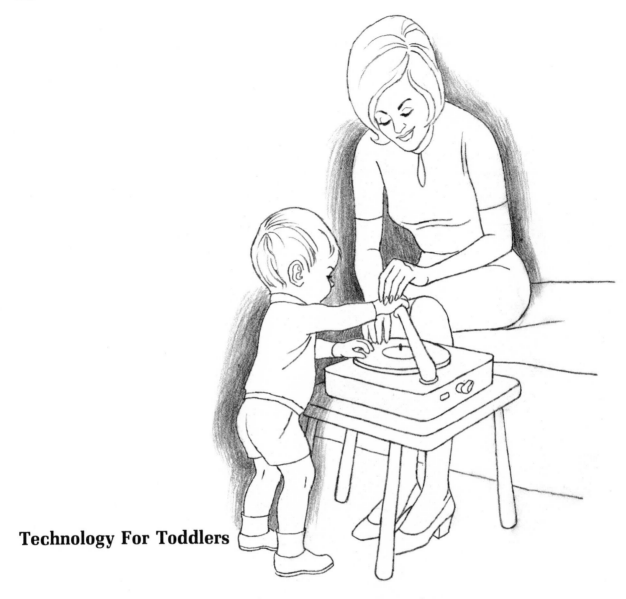

Technology For Toddlers

There are lots of activities you can devise to exploit your child's growing awareness of the technical world in which he lives. Two's can handle many pieces of equipment if you show them how and give them a chance.

They can turn on and off radios, television, and light switches; they can play tape recorders, and they can even handle typewriter keys. With care you can make these things interesting and fun rather than running scared with "no" and "don't."

Get a simple record player (45 RPM) with an on-off switch and plain needle arm. Buy some non-breakable records (or check them out from a library) and show your toddler how to play them. He can use the songs for background music; you can use them for round games.

Get a simple cassett or tape recorder. Show him how to record and listen. Talk into the mike and play it back. Let him try. Take turns, and then let him record your voices, his voice, music from the record player, a part of Sesame Street (or other TV show).

Show him how you can erase and re-use the tape or cassett.

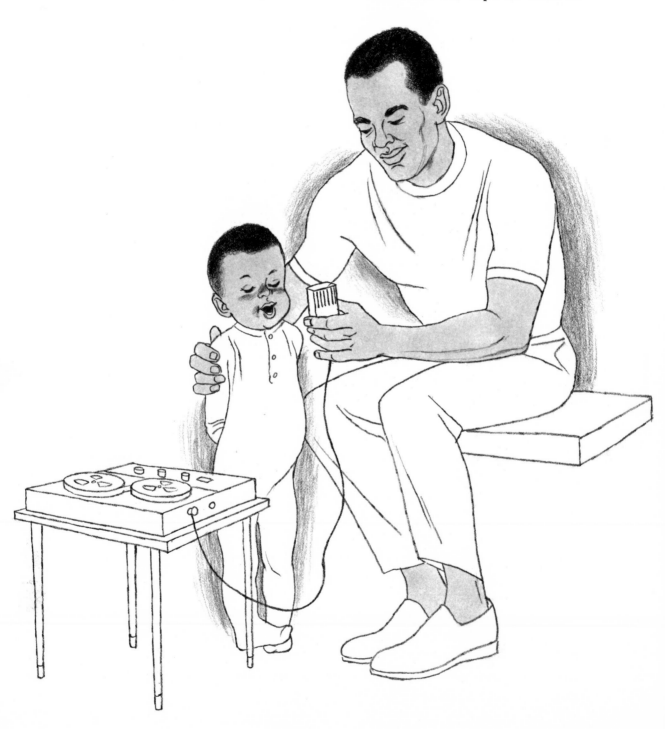

Let your child help and encourage him to help. He lives in a push-button world, and he might as well learn to push the right buttons.

As you go about daily activities, think of the ways he can help by pushing and pulling. If you live in a building with a self-service elevator, he can be held up to press the floor button. If you use a coin laundromat, he can put the coin in the slot and push it in, as well as helping you load the tumbler.

In the car, he can press door locks down and learn to buckle his seat belt or whatever contraption he's fastened in.

To you, all of these activities are routine—to him, they're new and exciting. Remember the world looks quite different through his eyes from the way it does through yours, and he'll be fascinated with the fact that the push of his finger makes some things go or stop. Of course, since he doesn't understand much about danger, you have to realize that discovery takes care—there may be some buttons you don't want pushed (like stove buttons!). At two he can learn the difference and will be willing to do so if there are things he *is* allowed to do.

CONCLUSION

This book has presented a variety of activites for stimulating the intellectual and personal development of a child between three months and two years of age. That's not, of course, all there is to child rearing. The usual topics such as discipline and toilet training have been purposely omitted. The focus here has been on games that are most likely to have a pay-off in self-esteem, security and intellectual growth. There are, naturally, any number of other activities that could be suggested. You've been urged throughout this book to think of your own ways of using the basic recipe to meet your skills and your child's own individual make-up.

What happens now? Intellectual development isn't like money in the bank. You can't count on what you've done to this point to carry the child through the rest of his life unless you continue to interact with him in appropriate ways as he grows. I hope the book has given you a principle as well as a set of techniques.

The principle is that your child learns best, and learns not only how to learn but also that it is fun, when you provide him with a variety of interesting and challenging things to do. These things teach him that he can *do,* he can affect his world, he is competent. With these basic building blocks of skill and self-confidence, additional experiences enable him to build his ability to learn and continue his growth in skills. With the basic idea, you should continue to develop your own procedures in the years before school and even during school.

Your attitude remains continually important in his development. He needs to see that you have time for him, that there is a part of your day that belongs to him. He needs to see that you grant him more and more room to try (within safety) to experiment, to explore without so protecting him that you cut off chances for him to learn. He needs to see that you applaud his efforts and enjoy his achievements.

Your child is ready to join you in some social doings. Trips to the zoo, to the park, to the museum, to the library are all now within range. He'll learn something different from these trips each time he goes, and as he grows. Use such trips as materials for drawing, block play, imaginative play.

As his language increases, he can participate in the meal-time conversations of the family which can include discussions of what he has seen and done. His contributions will be limited, but talking together has been shown to be an important factor in later school achievement.

We have introduced reading material and have suggested the use of adult magazines as well as children's books. I haven't recommended that you "teach" your child to read. I have suggested surrounding him with the fact of reading, with the presence of materials, with the model of you as reader, and with the experience that what's in books is interesting to see and know. Too many parents might get over-anxious and attempt to give the child formal lessons. Let him set his own pace. You may discover that sometime during the next two years he'll ask you what words are, or he'll surprise you by recognizing words that he's seen in the store and on television. This is a natural approach to reading and is the one best used by parents. He may want to learn the alphabet, and he may ask about numbers. Never turn him off! Respond to his questions and his search for information. I've suggested throughout the book that you take many things in stride, learn to observe and learn to pace. The same thing applies in the years ahead.

If the community has resources, such as nursery programs that are well run and have an educational component, you may want to try them in the next year or so. If your home is a good learning center and your child has opportunities to be around other children, the nursery school may serve merely as a supplement to home. Don't see entry into nursery school as preparation for Harvard. If your child goes and enjoys it, looks forward to it, then it's probably worthwhile to him.

I hope that you have learned from this book that being a parent can be the most worthwhile experience there is. It need not be a chore and a burden, it need not be approached with dread. It offers you a great opportunity to learn and live in new ways, and to aid your child to learn and grow.